Alayna the Cat

By Blaine Short

As afternoon fades into dusk, Alayna the cat races around the house. She is full of excitement because she gets to spend the night with her grandparents.

Alayna lives with her mom, dad, and sister Kaelyn. Her family loves each other very much.

However, her parents are going out tonight and that means a sleepover at Memaw's and Pappy's house. Visits to her grandparents are Alayna's favorite thing to do.

After supper Alayna and her sister pack their bags. They pack pillows and blankets, combs and toothbrushes, and Alayna's favorite stuffed fish.

It was a short walk to Memaw's and Pappy's house. Ten minutes later the family arrived at their front door.

Alayna and Kaelyn race to hug their grandparents. The girls leap into their arms and then they all go inside.

As the girls settle into playing a game with Memaw, Mom and Dad give hugs and kisses and say their goodbyes.

After a snack of milk and cookies it is time for bed.

Alayna and her sister brush their teeth, Memaw combs their fur and Pappy reads a bed time story.

The girls curl up on the living room floor. Pappy and Memaw say good night, and they turn out the light.

Alayna looks around the dark room and began to see unfamiliar dark shapes. Memaw's and Pappy's house had become a scary place. Alayna began to cry.

"What's wrong my little kittens?" Memaw asks as she rushes into the living room.

Memaw turned the light on while Alayna explained how the dark scared her.

"Can we keep the light on Memaw?" Alayna pleaded. "Okay, but it's very bright," Memaw whispered.

Alayna laid her head down but Memaw was right. It was too bright to sleep and Kaelyn began to stir beside her.

"You're right Memaw, but what am I going to do in the dark?" Alayna whimpers. "Let's try this," Memaw comforted as she gave Alayna a small old flashlight.

"Oh, thank you Memaw," Alayna replied sounding relived.

Memaw said goodnight and turned the light out. Alayna flicked on the flashlight and laid her head down.

Just as Alayna closed her eyes the flashlight began to flicker. The room became very dark and scary as the flashlight went out.

"MEMAW! PAPPY!" Alayna cried.

Pappy appears this time and turns on the light. "Are you still scared Alayna?" Pappy asks.

"Yes, my flashlight quit working," Alayna answers.

"Okay let's try this," Pappy says and pulls out a nightlight.

Pappy goes over to the wall and plugs in the night light, but it doesn't turn on. "Well, I guess it's just too old," Pappy says sadly.

"What am I going to do Pappy?" Alayna whines.

"AH! I have one more idea," exclaims Pappy.

He goes to the window and opens the curtains. The moon is full and the stars are bright. They light up the whole living room.

"You see my little kitten; only in the dark can you see the heavens light. So you can sleep under the stars tonight." Pappy tells Alayna. Alayna looks around as her eyes adjust and she is not scared anymore.

Alayna puts her head down on her pillow and stares at the stars. In a few minutes she is fast asleep. Pappy tucks the little kittens in and goes off to bed.

Night drifts on and the kittens are carried away with their dreams. Alayna and her sister sleep soundlessly until the morning light.

THE END

Made in the USA
Middletown, DE
31 October 2025